Ready, Set, Write

A HARRIS HUME ORIGINAL, MARCH 2018

ISBN 978-09997772-4-4

Printed in the United States of America

Designed by Imogen Ward

www.harrishume.com

"QUALITY IS NOT
AN ACT, IT IS
A HABIT."

-ARISTOTLE

"When everything works best, it's not because you chose writing but because writing chose you. It's when you're mad with it, it's when it's stuffed in your ears, your nostrils, under your fingernails. It's when there's no hope but that."

-Charles Bukowski

THIS BOOK IS FOR WRITERS

While many of the exercises in this book touch upon fiction, this book isn't just for fiction writers. It's for all writers who want to dedicate more time to writing. Whether you're a fiction writer, a memoirist, a poet, a journalist, or some sort of writer that there's no name for (yet), there's something for you in Ready, Set, Write.

FIVE MINUTES

If you're reading this book it's because you want something—to write more often, to hone your skills, to develop a regular writing habit. Over the next 90 days we're going to work together to achieve your writing goals, with me acting as your virtual coach and personal cheerleader.

Your job is to write.

Five minutes, each and every day. That's all I'm going to ask of you. Five minutes of nonstop writing, no matter where your mind goes or whatever writer's block arises. Even if you keep writing the same word over and over, you have to keep at it for five minutes straight.

The prompts and exercises in Ready, Set, Write are designed to keep you writing for those five minutes—and hopefully longer. That's why so many are in genres such as fantasy, weird fiction, and sci-fi, so that they may challenge you and your imagination. Whether these genres come naturally to you or not, let them be a way for you to explore new ideas.

THE EXERCISES

Throughout READY, SET, WRITE you'll encounter eight different kinds of writing exercises. Here's a primer on what to expect from them as you go through your writing journey:

FIRST LINE

First Line exercises are meant to act as the first line in a paragraph or story. Your task is to continue that story in any manner you like. Pay attention to tense (past, present) and person (1st, 3rd) to make sure you're consistent with what's presented in the first line.

CONCEPT

A Concept prompt will provide you with an idea to consider. You can write a story that reflects this idea or you can freewrite about the idea itself, exploring nuances within it or posing questions about it. Concept prompts often feature ideas with widespread ramifications.

ONE WORDER

As the name suggests, One Worder exercises focus on a single word intended to invoke thought or emotion. It's recommended that you consider the word for 30-60 seconds before you begin to write.

WWYD

WWYD or "What Would You Do?" exercises require you to answer a personal question or consider a hypothetical situation. They are meant to help you draw details from your life to make your writing more relatable.

RORSCHACH

Rorschach exercises are visual inkblot prompts designed to tap into your subconscious. You can either focus on the inkblot for 30-60 seconds before writing or give a brief (1-2 second) glance, letting your mind fill in the gaps.

TRIPLET

When you encounter a Triplet prompt, you will be given three words that you must use in your writing or, for an extra challenge, in the first line of your writing. These words are meant to contrast and compare with one another in surprising ways.

CREATOR

The Creator exercise puts you in the position of world-builder and lore-crafter, giving you a story element that you must develop according to the prompt's specifications. In this exercise you are strongly encouraged to avoid tropes and clichés.

FORMAT

Format exercises focus on the format of your writing, requiring you to structure your writing as dictated by the prompt. This can range from faux newspaper articles to vocabulary limitations to narrative rules.

SHARING IS CARING

Writing is a solitary pursuit but it doesn't have to be a lonely one. As you make your way through Ready, Set, Write, share your progress on social media by using the hashtag #readysetwrite and don't hesitate to tag me (@michaelalwill on Twitter and Instagram) so that I can personally cheer you on. Not only will people's support keep you going when you begin to lag, but by regularly sharing your work you'll develop a sense of accountability that will keep you going throughout Ready, Set, Write and beyond.

Ready, Set, *Write*

Day
1

Day 1. You're here. You made it. And today you begin a journey that will transform you into a better writer.

This first set of writing prompts are each of a different type to expose you firsthand to the exercises you'll be working with throughout this book. When you're done with a prompt, check the box in the bottom right corner of the page. Remember, at the very least give each prompt five minutes of nonstop writing, no matter what.

Good luck!

There is nothing as tempting in the world as a locked door.

Write about the most frightening moment in your life.

Maze

Rorschach

People all over a small portside city start turning into cats.

*Emerald * Cellar * Discover*

Day
7

Day 7. We're going to cap off your first week of writing with a new exercise type called the Creator prompt. As mentioned in the introduction, this prompt challenges your world-building skills and encourages you to put your own spin on designing the items described in the prompt.

For an extra challenge, try going through each Creator prompt several times to push your creativity to new heights.

Create an artifact that grants its wearer an uncanny amount of luck.

Concept

A priest faking the faith brings a woman back from the dead.

A stranger with my daughter's face was knocking at the door.

You are given the opportunity to call yourself one year ago, with 15 seconds to talk. What do you say?

I waited for her as long as I could. That's what I told everyone, anyway.

*Ribbon * Trenchcoat * Forget*

Host

Concept

A small band playing at a roadside dive discovers that their music draws strange creatures from the wilderness.

Day
15

Day 15. You're two weeks in. For many, this is where it gets difficult to keep up the daily writing habit. You might skip a day—perhaps you already have—but don't let that discourage you. If you're struggling, try sharing your writing on social media using the hashtag #readysetwrite for feedback and encouragement.

No one could hear it except for me.

You are given the choice between being able to talk to animals or plants. Which do you choose? Why?

The moon stops rotating one day and begins cracking open to reveal...

Rorschach

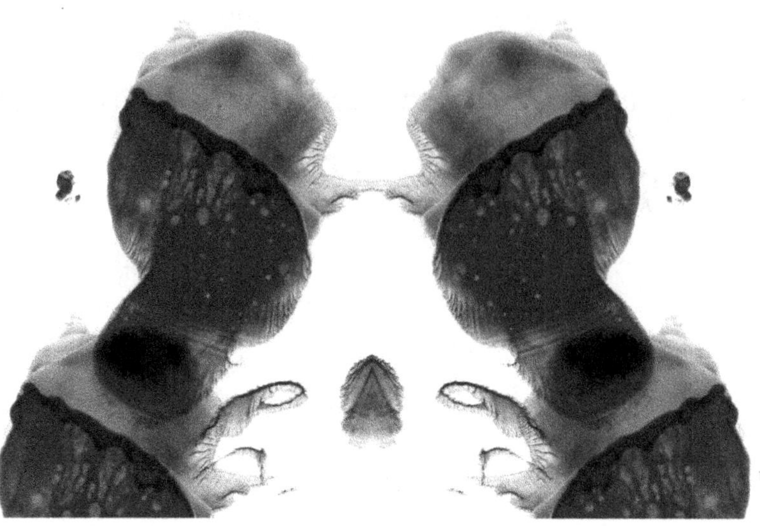

We didn't call it magic, not anymore. Not since the flood.

*Anchor * Salt * Seethe*

First Line

There were auras in my eyes again, iridescent constellations that told me I was about to change.

Concept

A woman goes looking for her high school sweetheart at his old address in their old town, but instead finds a twin of his she never knew about.

If you had a choice, what would you dream about tonight?

Dynasty

First Line

We called him Jack the Heart Attack. He was my brother and I hated him.

First Line

The room smelled of iron and sweat.

If you could read minds, whose mind would you read first and why?

First Line

They've got her, he thought. And now they're coming for me.

Concept

A transatlantic flight loses contact with ground control, forcing the flight to continue only on instruments. When they land the passengers and crew realize it is 100 years in the future.

Day 30

Day 30. At the end of this next set of exercises, you will find yet another new exercise type: the Format prompt.

Format prompts require you to follow a set structure and for the last exercise of this section, you will be asked to write six-word stories. A six-word story is just that, a full story told in just six words. The most famous six-word story was written by Ernest Hemingway. Here it is:

"For sale: baby shoes. Never worn."

Can you top that?

Rorschach

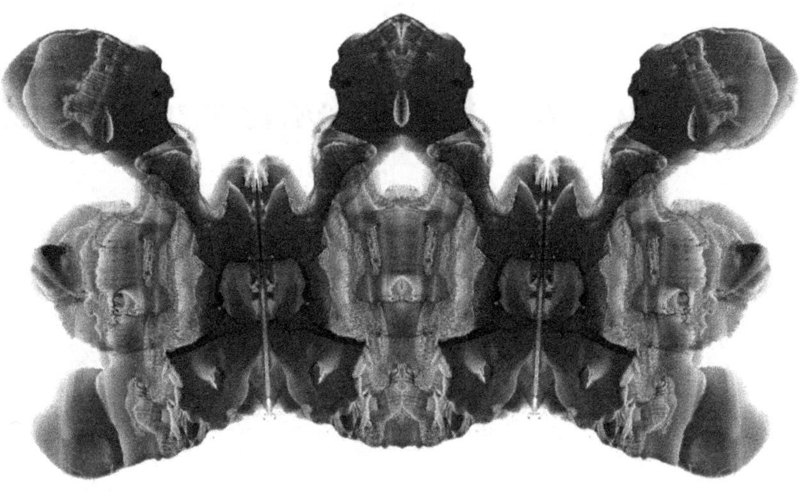

What was the last thing you regretted?

First Line

My uncle was the only one who survived the crash, but for those who knew him that was hardly a surprise.

First Line

Helen emerged from the basement, clothing soaked and eyes on fire.

Sweat * Star * Wander

First Line

It was the day Harold had been waiting for: he was finally going back to Earth.

Create a creature that feeds on shadows. Make sure to name it and to detail its environment and habits.

Concept

In Manhattan exists a bar that only seats three, its location changing every night.

Tunnel

First Line

That summer seemed to last forever.

Describe a time when you stood up for someone else.

First Line

They came to me on the anniversary of my son's death and asked if I had reconsidered their offer.

Teeth * Abyss * Dance

Concept

A woman wakes up to find a clone of herself in the same bed, still asleep. On her nightstand is a note that reads: "3 hours left."

Write 10 six-word stories. They must not relate to each other.

Day 45

Day 45. Welcome to the halfway point of this workbook. Take a deep breath, pat yourself on the back, and consider all the work you've done so far. You should be proud of the progress you've made.

We're going to start the second half of this book with a week of First Line prompts to seed ideas for you to develop into longer pieces. For an extra challenge, commit to turning one of these First Line prompts into a full short story of at least 2,000 words.

First Line

Her mother had finally found out.

As Rhine lay bleeding on the steps of the monument, he had an idea.

They were headed back home for the last time.

First Line

You think you know, but you don't. The hero I was—the hero they say I was—they only say that because I won. But I shouldn't have.

The mountain was breathing.

First Line

She spread her wings and leapt off the Empire State Buillding.

First Line

We brought out a blanket and dinner and the loveliest bottle of wine we could find to watch the end of the world from our backyard.

Rorschach

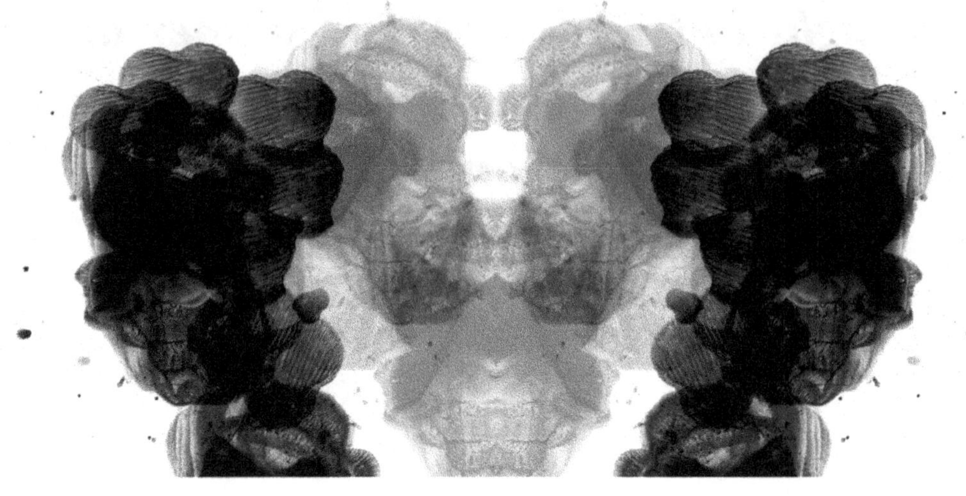

Concept

A research division of a technology company opens a facility in the middle of South Dakota, where they are rumored to be predicting the future.

What makes you angry?

First Line

She named herself Failure as a joke, not as a prophecy.

First Line

Sam waited twenty years to write her back.

Write about something you once broke.

First Line

The safecrackers arrived too late.

I'll give you two options, he said to me. "Shoot me or—" I pulled the trigger before he could finish his thought.

Day 60

Day 60. Before you jump into the next exercise, I want you to go back through your first two weeks of prompts. What was your writing like? What themes did you gravitate towards? Jot down a few notes on this page and take note of any prompts you found especially challenging (and why).

At some point in the next two weeks, turn one of the following exercises into a continuation of a prompt from your first two weeks. It can be a direct continuation, a different point in the same narrative, or a completely new perspective on an idea you've previously considered.

Concept

A dog begins showing up in a couple's backyard, but only at night. It appears to be friendly and when the couple goes to greet it, it seems to want to lead them into the woods.

First Line

We should have left that house before Dad discovered what we'd done.

*Spider * Cloud * Animate*

Concept

The hedonistic heir to a business mogul's fortune wakes up with a dead woman in his bed. Suddenly there is a knock at the door.

Write about a time you got lost.

If you could meet your 7-year-old self and tell them something, what would it be?

*Cue * Artist * Drive*

Concept

An unfathomably large sea creature washes ashore on a crowded beach. Etched onto its skin is a serial number.

If you could have any superpower, which would it be and why?

First Line

On Saturday he became dictator, which was nowhere near as fun as he thought it would be.

*Bottle * Eye * Throw*

First Line

Ashley wasn't happy about it, but her model had been recalled for a reason.

Concept

After a retired bodyguard is approached with a lucrative job offer, he must grapple with the mistakes that lead to the death of his last employer.

WWYD

You wake up with a new pet that takes the form of the animal your personality most resembles. What pet do you wake up with? Why?

Concept

In the future, the wealthy begin to rent bodies from younger, poorer individuals. One of these procedures goes awry and a rental comes to inhabit the body of a wealthy magnate.

Day 75

Day 75. We're almost there! Just two weeks left!

You'll have two Rorschach prompts before we get to Day 90 and I want you to try something different with each one of them. For the first one, give it just a glance—only a second or two—and then cover it up before writing. For the next one, study it intently for an entire minute and then begin your writing. Consider the differences in both approaches and how you adjust your writing when you have more or less information.

First Line

Aliens arrive on earth with a dire message: they are being pursued by a predator.

First Line

Myth, religion, faith—we told them all it was a fraud because it was the only way for them not to find out who we really were.

Rorschach

First Line

They had to make sure the nuns didn't notice.

Synthesize

Scar

WWYD

You get to go back to high school for one day, with all your current memories intact. You cannot change the future but you can behave however you would like. What do you do?

Triplet

*Mace * Gate * Lure*

Create a powerful weapon that curses those who wield it.

You are offered the chance to move anywhere and live there for 5 years. Where do you go and why?

Only the very oldest of us could still remember being able to hear.

It never occurred to my mother that I was not her child.

Oh Daniel, with his art fetish—or so I thought.

First Line

Someone must have seen her, because the Blindscouts were knocking at her door.

Rorschach

Day 90

Day 90. Congratulations! You're one day away from the finish line. Think about who you were as a writer when you started this book and think of how far you've come since then. All with five minutes of effort a day.

At some point after you complete today's exercise, I encourage you to go back through the rest of the book and pick out your top 5-10 favorite pieces of writing. These will be your seeds that you develop further and possibly even workshop. As we did on Day 45, I challenge you to turn at least one of these seeds into a story of 2,000 words or more.

First Line

The song floated in from the swampland, from down in that pit where no man lived. I knew the song and I knew what that meant for me.

NOW WHAT?

Congratulations again on completing Ready, Set, Write: Level 1! If you're wondering what steps you should take next on your writing journey, here are some suggestions:

- For more structured writing exercises, check out Ready, Set, Write Levels 2, 3, and 4.
- For writing guides, I absolutely recommend Stephen King's essential writing book, On Writing, as well as William Zinsser's On Writing Well. These books have similar names, but cover wildly different material. Both are fantastic.
- In general I recommend making a habit out of reading—specifically books in the genres or fields you wish to write in. It's hard to know your market if you don't know what they're reading.
- I also urge all writers to set themselves a goal, whether that's submitting to a literary magazine, writing a book, or even setting up a blog with regular posts. Be sure to give yourself a deadline.

Whatever your next step is, the most important thing is this:

KEEP WRITING

www.ingramcontent.com/pod-product-compliance
Lightning Source LLC
LaVergne TN
LVHW061332060426
835512LV00013B/2614
9780999777244